Creating a
Business Plan

Pocket Mentor Series

The *Pocket Mentor* Series offers immediate solutions to common challenges managers face on the job every day. Each book in the series is packed with handy tools, self-tests, and real-life examples to help you identify your strengths and weaknesses and hone critical skills. Whether you're at your desk, in a meeting, or on the road, these portable guides enable you to tackle the daily demands of your work with greater speed, savvy, and effectiveness.

Books in the series:

Leading Teams
Running Meetings
Managing Time
Managing Projects
Coaching People
Giving Feedback
Leading People
Negotiating Outcomes
Writing for Business
Giving Presentations
Understanding Finance
Dismissing an Employee
Creating a Business Plan

Creating a Business Plan

Expert Solutions to Everyday Challenges

Harvard Business School Publishing

Boston, Massachusetts

Copyright 2007 Harvard Business School Publishing Corporation

Printed in the United States of America

14   13   12   11   10   9   8

Library of Congress Cataloging-in-Publication Data

Creating a business plan : expert solutions to everyday challenges.
    p. cm. — (Pocket mentor series)
  Includes bibliographical references.
  ISBN: 978-1-4221-1885-6 (pbk. : alk. paper)
  1. Business planning—Handbooks, manuals, etc. 2. Business—Handbooks,
manuals, etc. 3. Business enterprises—Finance—Handbooks, manuals, etc.
I. Harvard Business School.
  HD30.28.C73 2007
  658.4'01—dc22

                       2007021448

Contents

Test Yourself   109

A helpful review of concepts presented in this guide. Take it before and after you've read the guide, to see how much you've learned.

Answers to test questions   111

To Learn More   115

Further titles of articles and books if you want to go more deeply into the topic.

Sources for Creating a Business Plan   119

Notes   121

For you to use as ideas come to mind.

Mentor's Message: The Importance of a Well-Prepared Business Plan

Meet Marshall, a young entrepreneur. He has a great idea for a new technology that he thinks will revolutionize the consumer goods industry. To get the business off the ground, he knows he'll need investment capital. Now meet LaNita. She runs a successful business but wants to apply for a loan so she can expand her enterprise. Finally, meet Paul, a brand director at a major company. He has an idea for a new product line and wants to get approval and funding from the firm's management team to develop the line.

Marshall, LaNita, and Paul each need a well-prepared business plan. A business plan is like a road map that will help each of these individuals gain financial and other support for their enterprise or project. A business plan will also enable them to handle the opportunities and obstacles they will inevitably encounter as they move forward with their dream.

Every business—whether it's a start-up company, an expansion of an existing firm, a spin-off from a parent corporation, or even a project within an established organization—needs a business plan to navigate successfully through its own unique competitive environment.

Preparing a business plan is a time-consuming process, as a well-developed plan has numerous sections and comprehensive information. To prepare a business plan for your own business or project, you will need to think carefully about a number of key issues—such as who your customers and competitors will be, how much money you'll need to invest in the business, and what kind of payoff you have in mind (to name just a few!).

But all of this work is very worthwhile. Armed with a well-prepared plan, you stand a much better chance of obtaining the investment dollars and other forms of support you'll need to make your business succeed.

Linda A. Cyr, Mentor

Linda A. Cyr is a partner at Tapestry Networks, a company that brings leaders together for strategic dialogues that set the agenda for economic, social, and organizational change. Linda's career spans both academic and corporate settings. Most recently, Linda was an assistant professor at the MIT Sloan School of Management and the Harvard Business School, where she created and taught entrepreneurship and leadership courses for both MBA students and executives. Her research and teaching examined ways in which a company's network of internal and external affiliations affects its financial performance. She has published articles in *The Academy of Management Journal* and *Entrepreneurship Theory and Practice* in addition to authoring Harvard Business School cases spanning industries that include biotech, consumer products, technology, and fashion.

Creating a Business Plan: The Basics

Getting Started

Why have a business plan?

Every business and major project needs a business plan, a road map for meeting the expected and unexpected opportunities and obstacles the future holds and to navigate successfully through the business's unique competitive environment.

Preparing a business plan is *part* of the process of preparing for a business. A business plan is not simply a document that's written quickly, passed around once, and then relegated to some dusty shelf. It's not a slightly modified version of a standard template drawn from a how-to book or an Internet site. Preparing a business plan is an intensely focused activity. It's an activity that requires honest thinking about your business concept, the business opportunity, the competitive landscape, the keys to success, and the people who will be involved. You'll find that your analysis results in more questions than answers. So, the next step in the process is to do the research to answer those questions.

What's your purpose?

Depending on the size and state of your business or project, the process of preparing, developing, and writing the business plan can take some time to accomplish. And once you're finished, you should use and reuse your business plan often to see whether your critical assumptions about key success factors are becoming realities. So before you plunge in, think about some of the overarching issues that can help shape your preparation of the business plan. Start by asking yourself why you are preparing the plan and what you are trying to accomplish by this undertaking.

If your business plan is to serve as a proposal within the resource-rich environment of a large corporation, then certain sections of the business plan, such as the marketing or operations plans, could be short and less developed than other sections. But suppose you are in a resource-constrained environment and you are using the plan to raise money from venture capitalists. In this case, you should focus on the sections these readers might consider key, such as the opportunity itself, the competitive analysis, the management team, and the financial expectations.

Who's your audience?

Know who will be reading your plan and why. Different types of audiences (or readers) will look for different information in a business plan. If you are clear about who your readers will be, then you can provide them with the information they consider most important.

If your venture is within a large organization, then your plan will be directed toward the board of directors or a management committee making capital investment decisions. If your venture is entrepreneurial, then your audience may be lenders or investors. Lenders will be considering the riskiness of the loan as they look at payback periods and cash flow data. Investors, on the other hand, may want to know what the breakeven points are and what the return on investment will be; investors will be interested in the longer-term potential of the business.

What Would YOU Do?

Plan? What Plan?

KYLA WANTED TO apply for a loan so she could expand her sailboat business. Her goal was to secure enough funds to make a major capital investment and finance her move into a new market. The loan officer reviewed her statements that documented her business's cash flow and took notes as she described the growing demand for her high-end sailboats. He then asked for a copy of her business plan. Business plan? Why did she need a business plan when she already had a successful company—which she simply wanted to expand? How could she convince the loan officer to lend her money?

In all cases, a smart audience will be considering the value of your business according to not just the financials but the soundness of the plan as a whole—the opportunity in the market, the differentiated product or service you will offer, the people involved, the competitive landscape, and, most importantly, what the financial returns will be.

Ask yourself what you expect from each type of reader. Do you want a corporate stamp of approval or the active support of upper management? Do you want funding alone, or do you want connections with other investors or other business partners? Do you want a loan to be repaid, or are you willing to share ownership and profits?

What information will you need?

Before you begin to put the plan together, determine whether you have all the information you need. You may have to do some research first. For example, have you confirmed the necessary production costs for your product? Have you checked out options for office space? Is your competitor analysis complete and up-to-date? Have you selected the most appropriate legal structure for your business?

There are many sources for this kind of information—some are simple and inexpensive, and some take time and money to discover. Before hiring market research professionals, check these readily available resources:

- Your local library

- The local chamber of commerce

- The Internet—especially official sites, such as the Small Business Administration, the IRS, the Census Bureau, the Association of Small Business Development Centers, Standard & Poor's, and major business periodicals

- State departments of economic development

- Printed industry publications and professional journals

- Trade shows

- Your competitors

Steps for Determining Your Information Needs

1. **Review the elements of a basic business plan.** Look at the larger picture to determine which pieces are filled in and which pieces need more attention. Depending on your business venture, you may not need to devote as much attention to some parts of a business plan as others.

2. **Define the categories of information you need.** As you develop your business plan, you might find that you are focusing on your own business without stepping back to look at the broader picture of the competitive industry. For example, you may have all the information you need about producing your own product, but you don't know what your competitors' production costs are. This information is important to ensure the cost competitiveness of your product.

3. **Determine the critical information you have.** Don't waste your time and efforts on finished work. Checking that you have complete information on certain critical areas will allow you to devote your energies to those areas that need further work.

4. **Determine the information you need to retrieve.** Focus on the critical areas of information you need. Typically, these areas will be outside of your expertise. For example, if you are a marketer, then the finance or production information may be lacking. Get help to determine information needs. Since the gaps will generally lie in unfamiliar territory, find someone on your team or hire a consultant to guide you through the process of determining what and how much information you need in that region.

5. **Explore where and how will you get the information.** In many ways, access to information is becoming easier and easier. The Internet continues to grow exponentially, providing information at a keystroke. Use search engines to find the Web sites for government, industry, marketing, and company information.

What You COULD Do.

Remember Kyla's meeting with the loan officer?

Here's what the mentor suggests:

Even though Kyla already runs an established, successful company, she should take the time to prepare a business plan. A business plan is essentially a blueprint for your business, a detailed guide that outlines your business concept, the business opportunity, the competitive landscape, the keys to success, and the people who are, or will be, involved. Preparing and then writing a business plan is a time-consuming process but well worth the effort. It's an important sales tool to use when you want to borrow money or gather support to launch a new product or service.

Anatomy of a
Business Plan

The opening, body, and attachments

The most common business plan structure is to move from short, general summaries to more detailed explanations. Thus, the opening sections—the executive summary and the business description—are both brief overviews of the business. The body of the plan consists of more in-depth descriptions of the fundamental elements and concerns of the business—the *who*, *how*, *what*, and *where* of your business. The attachments at the end include the most detailed information—the financial data, management résumés, and so forth.

Typical structure for a business plan

Most business plans contain these components:

- Cover page and table of contents
- Executive summary
- Business description
- Business environment analysis
- Industry background
- Competitive analysis
- Market analysis

- Marketing plan

- Operations plan

- Management summary

- Financial plan

- Attachments and milestones

Of course, not all business plans follow this model precisely. A plan may combine some elements, add new sections, and eliminate others. However, the critical information your readers need to know for a particular business must be included.

For example, the business plan for Private Communications Corporation (PCC), which will be used as an example throughout this guide, has all the components listed above. Nevertheless, the marketing plan and operations plan have been combined into one section in PCC's plan.

Despite variations in the structure of business plans, all basic business plans comprise descriptions of the opportunity, the context, the managers, and the financial risk and reward.

Cover Page and
Table of Contents

Preparing the cover page

Make sure your cover page signals what's to come. The cover page is the first thing your audience will see; it's like a newspaper headline that gives readers the quick information they need to decide whether to pass over this story or to continue reading. To ensure a positive first impression, your cover page should:

- Have a clean, professional appearance

- Include the name of the business or project

- Give your name and contact information

- Display your company logo or emblem

Developing the table of contents

The next page of the plan, the table of contents, is another kind of headline for readers, letting them know at a glance what topics will be covered. Your readers will check the table of contents to see whether it is inclusive—that all the important topics are listed. They will also note the maneuverability of your plan—that is, how easy it is to flip through the plan and quickly find the sections they want to read.

Executive Summary

A N EXECUTIVE SUMMARY may be the only section a reader uses to make a quick decision on the proposal, so it should fulfill your reader's expectations. The executive summary is a concise presentation of the main points of the business plan; it is a kind of abstract that gives a brief overview of the business venture.

Including the right information

What information might you include in your executive summary? As succinctly as possible, the executive summary should describe the following:

- **The industry and market environment** in which the opportunity will develop and flourish.

- **The special and unique business opportunity**—the customer problem your product or service will be solving.

- **The key strategies for success**—what differentiates your product or service from competitors' offerings. Indicate how your company will be the first to market with the product or service, or how your company will have a more efficient distribution system than the competitors, or that you have acquired strategic partners in the venture.

- **The financial potential**—the anticipated risk and reward of the business.

- **The management team**—the people who will achieve the results.

- **The resources or capital being requested**—a clear statement to your readers about what you hope to gain from them, whether it is capital or other resources.

Formal executive summaries

In its most direct mode, the executive summary is a formal statement presenting the company facts. As part of a legal document, Private Communications Corporation's executive summary (called the Company Overview) is an example of the formal type.

Company Overview

Private Communications Corporation ("PCC") was incorporated under the laws of the State of Florida on November 8, 2007. Its headquarters are located in Berkeley, California. The Company was formed for the purpose of developing and marketing a unique phone service product, more specifically described below. The Company has filed a petition with the Internal Revenue Service seeking to qualify as an "S Corporation" for tax purposes, in accordance with relevant provisions of the Internal Revenue Code. Although the

continued

Company anticipates that it will qualify, it has yet to receive confirmation of approval.

The Company was founded by Edward R. Defty and Andrew P. Laszlo, who, along with Paul Hoff and Ann Meceda, are actively managing the Company. The management team, together with certain members of Cohen, Berke, Bernstein, Brodie & Kondell, P.A., a commercial law firm located in Miami, Florida, own 100% of the Company's issued and outstanding common stock.

The Company has developed a unique product (the "Product") which is designed to permit people to talk and socialize over an ordinary telephone, with complete anonymity and privacy. People can converse openly, yet without having to reveal their phone numbers, true identities, or other personal information. The Product is being targeted initially at users of online chat rooms and online and offline dating services. Generally, it will be marketed through strategic alliances with proprietary online service providers (OSPs), Internet service providers (ISPs), chat rooms, and dating services. Additionally, the Company will promote the Product through targeted advertisements distributed over the Web and through more traditional print media.

The Company has scheduled the public launch of the Product for early April 2008, following the completion of a beta test, which is currently under way.

Executive summaries as mission statements

The purpose of the executive summary is to give the reader a quick understanding of the proposal, but it can also serve to capture the reader's interest in the business. This type of executive summary can function more like a movie trailer than a condensed abstract, to encourage the viewer to read on and see the whole picture. One component that can capture a visionary sense of the business is the mission statement. The mission statement should express the opportunity and business philosophy in one brief sentence.

For example, Private Communications Corporation's mission could be the following: "To provide the consumer with a unique telephone service that offers all the benefits of telephone communication while protecting the user's privacy."

Business Description

T HE BUSINESS DESCRIPTION is another summary, but it focuses more directly on the business concept itself by giving a brief yet informative picture of the history, the basic nature, and the purpose of your business. It should state clearly what the business objectives are and why the business will be successful.

Introducing your business

The business description gives you the chance to introduce your business in terms of its unique qualities and the positive business environment existing for your product or service. Here you can give pertinent background information that makes it clear why your concept is exciting, and you can express your commitment and capacity for making the business succeed. Thus, the purposes of the business description are to:

- Express clearly your own understanding of the business concept

- Share your enthusiasm for the venture

- Meet readers' expectations by providing a realistic picture of the business venture

Incorporating the right details

What goes into the business description? Include information about the business, such as:

- What the history of the concept or the business is (Is it on the drawing board, at the start-up stage, ready to expand?)

- What markets the business will serve

- What kind of business it is (manufacturer, retailer, service business)

- What the product or service is

- Why people will use it (What problem will the product or service solve for customers?)

- What the financial status is

You may decide to also include the following information:

- Who will manage the business (be sure to emphasize the skills and experience of the management team, as readers familiar with the industry will be most interested in the quality of the people on the team)

- What the structure of the business is (partnership, corporation, affiliate)

- Where the business will be located

Tip: Be enthusiastic in your business description. This is the section in which you present the value of your concept—why you believe the business will be a resounding success.

Highlighting your product or service

In some cases, the product or service is so unusual or technical that it deserves its own separate section to explain what it is and how it functions. A separate section will highlight for readers the offering's special features and unique points of differentiation.

For example, following the business description, Private Communications Corporation provides an in-depth product description as well.

Product Description

The Company has developed a unique telephone service that enables consumers to engage in two-way telephone conversations, using ordinary telephones, without either party having to risk disclosing their true phone numbers.

PCC's first product, directReach, will be launched in April 2008. Employing a sophisticated switching system and proprietary software, the Product will enable customers to receive telephone calls on any designated telephone line, through a toll-free number and private extension. The Product provides three important benefits that address the target end user's needs: privacy, flexibility, and convenience.

The Product is a full-featured call-management service that supports multiple extensions, several call-handling options, and voice mail. When a customer establishes an account, he or she is granted a personal extension number that can be assigned to a specific telephone number, such as a home, office, or cellular number. By giving others the extension number, in conjunction with the directReach toll-free number, the customer can receive phone calls and engage in totally private, anonymous telephone conversations.

The service is fully customizable, allowing the customer to configure the service to meet his or her unique needs. The user controls all Product features through a complete management system on the Web or through an easy-to-use Interactive Voice Response (IVR) telephone interface. Through this control system, the customer can easily:

- Register and activate the product using a credit card
- Specify the receiving number, and modify that number at any time

continued

- Program different receiving numbers for different times
- Terminate an extension and obtain new extensions
- Customize voice mail and check for new messages
- Review account usage and change monthly calling plans

The software programming and product design are proprietary to PCC. This allows the Company to offer such important features as ease of use, flexibility, and convenience for both the caller and the customer. With access to all features through an easy-to-use interface, the customer can have complete control over the calls he or she receives. The ability to change a number of calling options allows customers to adapt the service to their schedules and needs each day. In addition, customers and their acquaintances may call one another at any time, without having to first prearrange or coordinate a call.

Tip: In drafting the business description, balance your enthusiasm for the venture with a measured acknowledgment of the risks and costs involved.

Business
Environment
Analysis

U NDERSTANDING THE INDUSTRY, the competition, and the market in which your business will grow is fundamental to the development of a robust business plan. Your study will show that you have identified a real opportunity that solves a real customer problem. The result of the analysis will:

- Provide you with a thorough understanding of the business environment

- Guide you in developing an effective marketing plan

- Convince readers of the realistic potential of your business venture

The purpose of the business environment analysis is to show readers what the business opportunity is in this industry and market. What is the problem you are solving for the customer? What pain are you easing? What special technology, new perspective, or unique concept will you offer customers that will induce them to purchase your product rather than your competitors'?

Understanding industries and markets

Market is often used to describe the various elements of the total business environment. Here, however, the terms *industry* and *market* are used to describe separate but overlapping parts of the broader business environment. The industry is the group of companies that produce and sell products or services to the market. The market is where your product or service will be sold. The industry defines both your colleagues and your competitors; the market determines your opportunity and your customers. The area of intersection represents your business opportunity—that space in which the customer need and the product or service meet.

INDUSTRY *n* **1:** The group of companies that produce and sell products or services to a particular market

---

Asking the right questions

To analyze the business environment, ask these questions:

- **What is the industry?** What characteristics define the industry? For example, does the industry manufacture shoes, including running shoes? Produce software for computer training? Provide temporary employment services for businesses?

- **Who are your competitors within that industry?** What companies sell the same or similar products or services to customers within your market? What companies sell other offerings that meet the same needs your proposed product or service will meet?

- **What is the market?** For example, your market could be geographically defined as Boston or Paris, or it could be demographically defined as the teen market, the marathon-runner market, or the computer-user market.

- **Who are your customers within that market?** Are you selling a product directly to teenagers themselves? To their parents? To apparel retailers selling to teens?

You provide answers to these questions in the industry background, competitive analysis, and marketing analysis sections of the business plan.

Tip: In doing the research for your business environment analysis, check the most accessible sources first. That way, you won't get overwhelmed by all the information out there. And you'll stay focused on finding the information you need for your business venture.

Industry Background

T HE INDUSTRY BACKGROUND section provides your readers with information to understand the shape, size, trends, and key features of the industry and to understand how your product or service will fit into that industry.

Defining existing products and services

What are the products or services currently produced by the industry? To provide this information in the industry background section of your plan, ask yourself questions such as:

- What is the range of products or services encompassed by this industry?

- Is it an electronics industry or a television-manufacturing industry?

- Is it a food industry or a cereal-making industry?

Sizing the industry

What is the size and shape of the industry? Ask questions such as:

- What is the industry's production capacity, its unit sales, and its overall profitability?

- Is the industry spread out geographically, or is it concentrated near the sources of raw material or near the end user for efficient distribution?

Identifying important trends

What are the important trends emerging in the industry? To identify them, ask:

- What is the predicted growth rate?

- What new patterns of growth are emerging?

- What factors might contribute to future growth?

- Is the industry fragmented, consisting of many small competitors?

- Are a few major competitors controlling the industry?

- Is it moving quickly on the edge of technology, or is it a traditional industry offering stable products or services?

Tip: In identifying important trends, document your sources. Good record keeping at the research stage will pay off in the short and long term.

Anticipating barriers to entry

What are the obstacles that could block you from entering this industry? To anticipate these barriers to entry, ask:

- What resources, knowledge, or skills does it take to enter this industry?
- Are there restrictive federal or international regulations, large capital requirements, or areas of sophisticated technical knowledge associated with providing the products or services?

In Private Communications Corporation's case, the industry background provides a brief history of the recent phenomenon of chat rooms on the Internet. To indicate the growth potential of the PCC business, entrepreneur Andy Laszlo describes the rapid development of the chat room and other possible niches, such as dating services.

Industry Background

Starting in 1995, Internet usage began its rapid ascent in popularity, owing in part to the introduction of user-friendly browsers that made accessing the World Wide Web (the "Web") easy and inexpensive. Other factors fueling the rapid growth in Web usage included the large and growing installed base of PCs, advances in the performance of PCs and modems, and improvements in network infrastructure. Web usage had grown from 1 million users in late 1994 to roughly 170 million users by 2006.[1]

Chat rooms were one of the earliest applications on the Web to gain popularity. Chat rooms were virtual communities where people could hold anonymous conversations with other participants by typing out their comments on their computer keyboards. Some sites were totally dedicated to chat, while others offered separate chat rooms as part of their sites.

For example, the ESPN Web site offered a number of different chat rooms where participants could discuss specific sports-related topics with players or game analysts. Search engines also began offering users the opportunity to chat about a number of general topics at any time, in addition to providing scheduled discussions with soap stars, authors, and other celebrities.

Many chat rooms also allowed users to move into "private chat rooms" to hold more private conversations. America Online (AOL), the largest online service, hosted more than 1 million hours of chat per day through some 14,000 chat rooms.[2]

Many Web sites were adding chat rooms in an effort to build a sense of community around their sites, which in turn was believed to be a key driver behind generating traffic at a site. In fact, studies demonstrated that adding a chat room to a Web site could boost traffic by as much as 50 percent, and users of chat rooms stayed on a site over four times as long as non–chat room users.[3] Many industry analysts projected that chat room usage could grow even faster than Internet usage. One leading analyst projected that there would be 7.9 billion hours of online chat by the year 2006.[4]

In addition to chat rooms, online match services had also become quite popular. These services enabled participants to submit

continued

personal profiles and search a site's database for the personal pro-files of other participants to find potentially interesting partners. Some sites were entirely dedicated to online matchmaking, whereas other sites offered match services as just one of many options. PCC estimated that there were well over 300,000 users of online match services in 2006.

As interest in chat rooms and match services grew, so too did concerns over personal privacy. Databases housing confidential personal information stored on computer networks could sometimes be accessed using only a person's Social Security number or telephone number. As concern increased, a number of companies had emerged to sell products to improve computer and telecommunications security.

[1] International Data Corporation.
[2] *BusinessWeek*, May 5, 2003.
[3] Ibid.
[4] *Advertising Age*, August 5, 2004.

Competitive Analysis

C OMPETITORS CAN BE companies within the industry producing similar products or services, such as motorcycles within the motorcycle industry. Or they could be companies in rival industries producing products or services that fall into another industry category but that solve the same consumer problem. For example, if the problem that's being solved is finding a low-cost alternative to owning and driving a car, then owning and riding a motorcycle or taking public transportation would both be competitive solutions. The readers of your business plan will want to know who the direct and potential competitors of your business venture are, because they represent a threat to the success of your venture. Understanding who your competitors are can reduce the risk of failure for your business.

Identifying your competitors

Who are your competitors? Think in terms of which companies solve the same problems for the customer that you intend to solve. Identify major competitors, their products and services, and their strengths and weaknesses. How much market share does each competitor control? What are their marketing strategies? What are their key success factors? Document all your responses in this section of your business plan.

Distinguishing your business from rivals

What differentiates your product or service from competitors' offerings? To answer this question, determine how you are responding to a customer need in a new, useful, and unique way. For example, if you plan to sell a product to consumers, will your product be much easier to use than similar offerings currently on the market? Or suppose you intend to provide a service to large companies: will your service help your client firms save more money or achieve greater efficiencies than your competitors' services could do?

Assessing threats from the competition

How much of a threat are your competitors to your venture? Do they enjoy strong brand recognition of their products? Will they aggressively block the entrance of a new rival? Will they recognize your special differentiating attributes and appropriate them for their own products or services?

Private Communications Corporation's competitive analysis identifies the competition and emphasizes PCC's competitive advantages—including convenience, flexibility, and strategic alliances.

What Would YOU Do?

Friend or Foe?

E ric was excited about his idea for a low-cost, easy-to-use software package that would help owners of small businesses handle their accounting. He had carefully analyzed trends emerging in the accounting software industry and was ready to prepare the competitive analysis section of his business plan. When he considered who might constitute his rivals, the obvious answers came immediately to mind—for example, existing software providers who already sold accounting packages. But Eric wanted to be sure that he was thinking as broadly as possible about potential competitors of his venture. The problem, though, was that he wasn't exactly sure of how to go about widening his "competitive lens."

Competitive Analysis

Direct competitors

To the Company's best knowledge, there is only a single competitor, PeopleLink Inc., that is presently offering a similar product. PeopleLink tested its product in October 2005 with a beta test that lasted several weeks. The company is promoting its product through a Web site that will permit people to establish new accounts and receive an extension number online. It is not known whether (and if so, to what extent) the system will be modified now that the beta period has been completed. PeopleLink is positioning its product as a "call conferencing system designed for chatters." It is advertising a general release date of winter 2007.

Although the Company has reason to believe that PeopleLink's price structure and marketing plans may be similar to those of the Company, PCC's Product is clearly distinguishable from, and more attractive than, PeopleLink's product. PeopleLink's product is essentially a private teleconferencing service. For two people to talk over their telephones using the PeopleLink system, they must both call into the same phone number virtually simultaneously (i.e., within a three-minute window). Otherwise, they cannot be connected. Thus, *PeopleLink's system requires users to prearrange and coordinate beforehand each and every call they wish to make.*

In contrast, *PCC's product is flexible and convenient, permitting people to call one another whenever they desire, without the need to prearrange contact.* Customers have complete control over where and when they answer their phone, and can direct calls automatically to voice mail if they do not answer the call or choose not to accept it. Management believes that its system is superior to that of PeopleLink and that its product differentiation will give the Company a material advantage over its competition.

Potential competitors

Generally, there are few natural barriers to entry (e.g., capital requirements, proprietary technology) that would prevent new market entrants from launching competing products. Consequently,

continued

prospective competitors will likely develop and promote competing products once they learn of the Company's success. Anticipating the threat of new market entrants, the Company is seeking to erect two strategic barriers to entry aimed at preserving the Company's competitive advantage. One barrier will arise through the formation of purposeful strategic alliances with those enterprises that maintain the gateways to chat rooms and dating services, such as OSPs, ISPs, chat room Internet sites, and dating services. The Company is presently negotiating advantageous revenue-sharing agreements with several potential partners, whereby the partners will promote and build services around the Company's product on an exclusive basis. The Company believes that these exclusive arrangements will effectively preclude potential competitors from reaching the Company's target markets in a cost-competitive fashion. Additionally, the Company is seeking to establish a second barrier by creating a brand identity for its Product so that consumers will come to recognize the Company's brand as a reliable service that ensures high-quality, convenient telephone communications with complete privacy and anonymity.

Internet telephony

Internet telephony is a technology designed to permit people to make long-distance phone calls, using either their personal computers or ordinary telephone handsets as receivers and the Internet as the communications channel. Generally, firms providing Internet telephony intend the technology to offer an alternative to ordinary long-distance telephone service, without any long-distance charge or for a charge substantially lower than the customary charge.

Moreover, Internet telephony supports anonymous long-distance telephone services, and some chat rooms incorporate Internet telephony features into their programs. To date, consumers have failed to embrace the technology. Many agree that the voice transmission is poor and, in most cases, is not real time. Furthermore, most Internet telephony software applications require that callers have compatible hardware and software to use the system. In short, the Company does not believe this technology poses a competitive threat in the immediate near term. However, should the technology improve and become a part of the PC mainstream, it could pose a substantial competitive threat to the Company's business.

What You COULD Do.

Remember Eric's problem?

Here's what the mentor suggests:

To think as broadly as possible about potential competitors for his business venture, Eric should ask himself who is meeting the same customer needs he plans to meet through his product or service. Anyone who meets those same needs is a competitor—even if they're in a totally different industry.

For example, through his accounting software, Eric hopes to offer a product that's easier for small-business owners to use than the complicated applications currently on the market. He thus intends to meet customers' needs for simplicity. Other software companies claiming to offer easy-to-use products would constitute his most obvious competitors. But tax accountants would also be rivals, since they, too, make accounting easier on business owners by handling all the paperwork. If Eric wanted to think even more broadly about potential competitors, he could consider pencil manufacturers as potential rivals as well. Why? Small-business owners terrified of complex software might decide to do their accounting the "good, old-fashioned way"—by working out the numbers themselves on paper! To attract these customers, Eric would have to convince them that his software was as easy to use—if not easier—than the lowly pencil.

Market Analysis

I N THIS SECTION, focus on your target market—that group of people or companies that will choose to purchase and continue to purchase your product or service because you solve a problem or meet a need for them better than your rivals do. Here is where you answer two questions: First, is there an opportunity within this market? Second, can we capitalize on this opportunity?

Assessing the market's size and growth

Indicate how large the market for your offering is and how fast it is growing. These are two key considerations for any business looking to enter a market or market niche. Is there room for your presence in that market? Can the market expand to include you? Will market demand for your products or services grow? For example, as consumers continue to appreciate the convenience of shopping online, companies will find more profitable opportunities to sell on the Internet.

Tip: Document your information. Your claims about market growth or competitor response should be supported by realistic and verifiable information.

Defining your target market

Who are your target customers—the individuals or companies to which you plan to sell your offering? Where are they from? What characteristics describe them? Consider the target market from different points of view, such as geographic location or segmentation (national, state, suburban, city, neighborhoods), demographic features (age, gender, race, income level, occupation, education, religion, etc.), and behavioral factors (customers' attitudes and responses to types of products).

Articulating your value proposition

Why will customers in your target market purchase your product or service? That's your value proposition. To define your value proposition, ask, What are your solutions to customer problems? What customer pain will your product or service ease? For example, do you have a better-designed pillow to ease back pain? Do you have a way to filter out banner ads on the Internet, easing online irritation? What are the benefits of your offering for those buyers? How will your customers differentiate your product from your competitors'?

VALUE PROPOSITION *n* **1:** The unique set of benefits your customers will get if they choose to purchase your offering over competitors' offerings

---

Private Communications Corporation's market analysis first defines the overall market for its business as "online and Internet communications" and describes the market size. Next, Laszlo focuses on the target segment of the market ("users of online chat rooms and dating services") and shows what the market need or opportunity is (privacy in telephone communications).

Market Analysis

Market definition

PCC competes in the arenas of online and Internet communications that facilitate the creation of personal relationships and/or allow for interactive communication between users. With proprietary online services, these arenas might include chat rooms, bulletin boards, and e-mail. On the Internet, they include Internet Relay Chat, e-mail, and various Web sites. The WWW sites of particular interest include those dedicated to real-time chat, those that support chat as an additional feature of the site, and those that serve to create online matches between users.

Total market size

Whereas the Web was essentially a novelty in the consumer marketplace just a year ago, the penetration of the Web during the last twelve months has been extraordinary. Although estimates vary, most authorities agree that the market consists of between 35 and 60 million Internet users. Where these users go, what they look for, and how long they spend on the Web are open questions that no one has yet been able to satisfactorily answer. Whatever the exact numbers and habits may be, there is unanimous consensus that the Internet is here to stay, and that the "cyberspace" it harbors will become an even more integral part of modern-day communications and social interactions in the twenty-first century.

Proprietary online service usage
While there is considerable variance in the estimated numbers of Internet users, usage of proprietary online services is more widely known through posted subscribership. Currently, the combined customer base of the three largest OSPs exceeds 50 million. All three OSPs offer proprietary content available only to subscribers, as well as complete access to the World Wide Web.

Target segment of the market
The initial target for PCC's Product is users of online chat rooms and dating services. These consumers share the desire to communicate with new acquaintances, and appreciate being able to remain anonymous and "selectively reachable" unless or until they feel the need to raise the level of intimacy.

Market need
By working longer hours, marrying later in life, and frequently moving to new locations, people have found it more difficult to build local social networks in their communities. At the same time, the Internet has made a virtual community of the entire world itself, so that people from different countries and cultures can now find and enjoy relationships with others who share their interests. Chat room

continued

discussions, computerized bulletin-board postings, and online personal ads and matching services are all utilized as a method to meet people and build relationships. And yet, to move the relationship to a more personal and intimate level, most people still feel the need to step away from the new technology and move their relationship to an old technology—the telephone. Taking that step, however, currently requires one party to abandon one of the most striking and comfortable features of the Internet—anonymity.

As consumers' embrace of the Internet and newly developed telecommunications media has grown, so too have their concerns over privacy and confidentiality. The Internet has made accessible powerful databases that contain some of the most private information about individuals. With just a phone number, even a lay person can learn volumes of personal data about somebody, while malicious hackers or stalkers can arm themselves with enough information to become extremely threatening or dangerous.

Estimated segment size
The market opportunity for PCC's communication services depends heavily on how one estimates current Internet and online services usage in general, and the use of chat room and dating services in particular. AOL estimates that 40 percent of its users visit its proprietary online chat rooms, a number that is likely similar for the other major services. A conservative estimate of the non-OSP Internet users who access chat rooms or utilize dating services is 10 percent. This yields a potential target market of 4.8 million OSP users and 2.3 million ISP users (using a conservative 35 million Internet

users minus the 12 million OSP users), for a total of 7.1 million target customers. With the current growth of Internet usage estimated at 50 percent per year, this number will reach over 20 million by 2008. Furthermore, chat is growing even faster than the Internet as a whole, as sites institute chat rooms as a way to create a "community" of regular visitors. Today, many companies provide chat rooms as a way to draw visitors to their sites. One analyst at Montgomery Securities estimates that by 2008, there will be 7.9 billion hours of online chat (*Red Herring*, July 2006). Dating services are also growing, with the largest claiming 100,000 members. Assuming they have 50 percent of the market, this segment alone currently has 200,000 highly qualified target customers.

Marketing Plan

YOU'VE EXAMINED THE business environment. You've studied the competition. You know your target market. You've discovered the opportunity. You have a product or service to sell. How do you bring your product and your market together? How can you encourage customers to buy from you? Typically, the most effective way is to develop, act on, and monitor a marketing plan.

Using your marketing plan as a road map

Your marketing plan serves as a kind of road map describing how you intend to sell your product or service—that is, how you will motivate the customer to buy. Developing and including a well-thought-out marketing plan in your business plan has two benefits:

- It helps you and your team pretest ideas, explore options, and determine effective strategies for the company's success.

- It helps convince your business plan readers of your own competency.

The plan should reflect the mission and basic business philosophy of your company. It should also incorporate and use the results of your market research.

Developing your marketing plan

How can you ensure that your marketing plan is coherent, that it pulls together all the elements of your business opportunity and philosophy? Start by looking at the key factors affecting the marketing of your product or service.

Specifically, *concentrate on the opportunity*—the customer problem that your product or service is solving. For example, you may be fixing a weakness in the competitors' services by offering customized service or guarantees on products that aren't available elsewhere. Or you may have discovered how to make low-fat foods taste like high-fat foods. As you develop specific marketing strategies, keep viewing the opportunity from the perspective of the customer.

Also, *review your marketing objectives*. At what level of sales will you reach the breakeven point—the point at which your sales cover your costs? When do you anticipate reaching that point? How long will it take to reach the next sales milestone? For example, your objectives might be to reach the breakeven in six months from the time of initial sales, to achieve a growth rate for sales of 10 percent per year, and to capture 10 percent of the target market in five years. What strategies can you design to fulfill these objectives?

In addition, *focus on customers' buying behavior*. When, where, why, and how do consumers buy this product or service? What needs are being fulfilled for them? What factors are important to them in choosing this type of product or service (for example, price, quality, value, benefits)? For a busy customer, service and time savings may be more important than the lowest price.

Finally, *determine each customer's value to your business*. Weighing the cost to acquire a customer with the long-term value of that customer helps you decide on the appropriate marketing strategies to use. For example, if each customer is worth winning and keeping, then the more expensive marketing strategies of relationship-oriented direct sales might be worth the cost. If, on the other hand, you are trying to reach a wide range of customers, then less expensive strategies, such as mass mailings of sales promotions, can be more effective. To determine the value of a customer, consider the following questions:

- Are you building an annuity business, such as magazine subscriptions that continue for years, or does your business provide a quick, one-time service?

- Do customers buy your product often as a consumable or inexpensive entertainment, or is your product durable—purchased only occasionally during a lifetime?

- Do you need to build brand loyalty, or is your product/service the only one that will fill customers' needs?

- Is the process of buying the product/service relationship oriented, requiring direct sales, or is it transaction oriented and easily adapted to direct-mail marketing or online selling?

Defining your marketing mix

Your marketing mix describes the way you will achieve your marketing objectives. Your choices define how you will make the target market aware of your product, how you will motivate the customer to purchase your product, how you will build customer loyalty for your product, and how you will achieve the projected return on sales. The strategies in your marketing mix determine the way you position your product in the market relative to your competitors' products. The most effective mixes reflect the classic "four Ps" of marketing: product, price, place (distribution), and promotion.

The first of the four Ps is *product/service*. Make sure that your product or service is consistent with your company philosophy and target market's needs. For example, if the company philosophy is to provide the highest-quality accounting services, then those services must be the most accurate and comprehensive available to wealthy customers, who require accuracy and comprehension from their financial services providers.

The second of the four Ps is *price*. At what price point will you offer your product or service? Will there be an established price, or will it be tiered or variable depending on consumer demand? Your pricing decisions will depend, on the one hand, on the price sensitivity of your market and the market's perceived value of your product. On the other hand, total costs and required profit margin also affect the price of the product. Pricing is difficult to predict. You will have a range of prices available determined by costs and expected contribution margins. However, within that range, you might adjust price in response to consumer demand.

The third P is *place.* The term *place* indicates the physical movement of products—how the product will be transported from the plant to the end user. What channels of distribution will you use? How will your product be merchandised—in what kind of retail store or location? These decisions depend on the type of product, the costs of distribution, and customers' needs or demands. You should make these choices in conjunction with other operating and marketing considerations.

The final P is *promotion.* Through promotion, you make consumers aware of your product. Promotion includes activities such as these:

- **Word of mouth.** This selling tool is the cheapest and most effective kind of promotion—satisfied customers spreading the word. However, it is unpredictable and difficult to control. If the word is positive, then your sales will increase, but a negative message is difficult to overcome.

- **Sales promotion.** In this case, you control the message by spreading the word to the consumer through coupons, samples, and demonstrations. A relatively low-cost program, sales promotion can reach a wide audience.

- **Direct sales.** Direct selling is more expensive than the general approach of sales promotions, but it is an important tool for developing relationships with customers while motivating them to buy. The tactics used in direct sales range from individual sales calls to mass telemarketing and broadcast e-mailing.

- **Advertising.** Advertising influences the consumer through paid persuasive messages delivered to the target market. This sales approach can be expensive, but the payoff is a strong brand image and brand loyalty.

Depending on your resources and whom you are trying to reach, select the interrelated mix of marketing strategies appropriate for your product or service and your target market.

Your marketing plan should fit with all the other pieces of the business plan, and it should show how you will achieve your specific marketing objectives. PCC's marketing plan is shown below.

Marketing Plan

PCC's marketing plan is based on the recognition that the customer may not always be the end user. The end user is the individual who is using the Internet or OSP to forge relationships that he or she wishes to take to a more personal level, but who is still concerned about anonymity or security. The customer, however, in some cases is the site or organization that provides the means for the forging of the end user's relationship. By encouraging the promotion of the Product by ISPs, OSPs, chat room sites, and online dating services, PCC gains access to their customers, who represent highly qualified prospects for the Product. This gives the Company two benefits: a

continued

less expensive and more efficient way to reach the end user, and a lock on the primary distribution channels that will help erect barriers to entry.

Positioning

To site partners, the Company is positioning the product as a value-added service for their members that can also significantly enhance their revenue stream. With ad revenue still a far cry from that of traditional media, and with the cutthroat pricing of the OSPs and ISPs, many service and content providers are hungry for additional revenue and are actively seeking partners that can provide it.

To end users, the Company is positioning the Product as a means to preserve one's anonymity, and thus guarantee security, while furthering relationships with new acquaintances encountered online. The Product facilitates these relationships without the pressure of a premature commitment and without requiring the user to make a snap decision about the risk of revealing personal information to a stranger. It also gives parents a safe way to allow their children to engage in the same type of offline personal relationships with new friends made online, without the risk of encountering adults with questionable intentions.

Pricing

The product is priced at only a moderate premium over standard long-distance telephone service, with a per-minute cost of between $.59 and $.79 incurred by the receiver of the call. This price is low enough that the customer should not feel restrained to release his or her number to prospective callers, and will not constantly be "watching the clock" while using the service.

There are monthly subscription plans that offer free blocks of time, discounted calls, and free access to premium features. Monthly plans will encourage regular usage of the service, as customers are likely to use the service at least enough to consume their "free" time. PCC is pursuing a value pricing strategy because it is the best way to create a community of long-term users who will incorporate the service into their daily lives instead of viewing and using it as a luxury entertainment product.

Remuneration to partners may take the form of revenue sharing, payment of a bounty for new subscribers, or guaranteed levels of paid advertising.

Customer value proposition
PCC is offering customers a superior benefit at a low cost. With the Company's service, customers can receive phone calls at their preferred location, on a schedule of their own convenience, with the flexibility to change or cancel their number at any time, and remain completely anonymous—all for nearly the same cost as making a standard long-distance telephone call. At the same time, these phone calls fill a need similar to that provided by chat rooms, but offer the additional value of being a more intimate and interactive form of communication. At the other end of the live/interactive spectrum, existing telephone services such as psychic talk and romance chat are significantly more expensive to use, often costing over $5.00 per minute.

continued

Strategic site and online service provider partners realize value by incurring a significant revenue stream at no, or very little, direct cost. Additionally, because site users will recognize value in the Product, hosting and promoting the Product becomes a means of differentiation for the site or service provider.

Distribution

The Product is targeted at Internet and online users. Therefore, the primary means of distribution will be via the directReach online informational and registration site. Users will be drawn to the site via banners and partner links. Other methods of reaching end users may include offering the Product in conjunction with a site's primary service, so that customers would, for example, obtain a directReach account when they establish a dating account or open an Internet access account with an ISP.

Customers are also able to join the service through a toll-free automated phone line. People wary of paying by credit card over the Internet could use this method, as could those drawn to the service via non-Internet means. In addition, all people calling a directReach member will be given the option of learning about the service, and becoming a member themselves, at the time they place their call.

Advertising and promotion

Advertising and promotion will be a three-phase process, involving public relations, Web and print advertising, partner acquisition, and brand imaging. Outside advertising and PR agencies will be utilized as much as possible in order to further ensure the creation and presentation of an overall coherent and professional message.

Phase I is expected to last ten to twelve weeks and involves acquisition of customers through print and Web advertising. Web banner ads will be placed on sites that offer chat services, with a click-through link to the directReach Web site. The directReach home page will present information about the service features, usage, and benefits, as well as an online registration form. Ads and site copy will strive to educate readers on the importance of maintaining personal security by not giving out phone numbers to strangers and will stress the three key benefits of the service. Moreover, the Internet ads will extol the excitement gained by moving an online chat to an offline phone call.

PR is also a major emphasis during Phase I, with special attention placed on targeting Internet publications and mainstream press with information about PCC's unique service. Press kits with promotional material and free trials of the Product will be sent to key reviewers and writers.

Phase II will begin concurrently with Phase I and involves acquisition of strategic partners. Primary targets are those establishments that already have relationships with the target user: OSPs, ISPs, and sites hosting chat rooms and dating services. Since potential partners may want proof of the concept before engaging in an agreement with PCC, Phase I must successfully demonstrate the reliability of the Product.

Phase III begins immediately after the successful implementation of Phases I and II and will emphasize the branding of the service,

continued

through newspaper and Internet advertising, billboard displays, and additional generation of media coverage. This type of promotion will be ongoing, with the primary purpose of strengthening the brand in order to build a solid customer base and deter the entrance of potential competitors. Significant resources will also be dedicated to building customer loyalty, through live operator service with well-trained and professional customer-service representatives, promotions and incentives for frequent users, and new and customized calling services. It is important that the brand consistently convey a message of legitimacy and professionalism, from advertising to customer service to product reliability.

Operations
Plan

Understanding operations

The operations plan gives an overview of the flow of the daily activities of the business and the strategies that support them. There should be enough information to show the reader that you understand and have planned for the daily execution of the business, but the plan should not be too technical or so comprehensive that the reader is either unable or unwilling to plow through it. The primary purpose of the operations plan section is to show that you are focused on the critical operating factors that will make the business a success.

Operations is the work of the business; it is the transforming of the ideas or the raw materials into products or services to be sold to the customer. The operations plan has to be as dynamic as the process of production itself. To continue as a vital guide for the action of the company, this internal plan can never lie quietly on some dusty shelf. It should be developed and used and modified as often as needed.

Determining breakeven point

The operations section of the business plan should give the reader the critical success factors affecting *how* the company creates value for the stakeholders of the business. The most important of these factors is the *breakeven point*—that is, the point at which unit sales equal operating costs. The breakeven point determines how many units of the product or service must be sold to break even, to cover the cost of producing the offering, so that the following units will produce a profit. Breakeven identifies the point at which the business will begin to make money.

BREAKEVEN POINT *n* **1:** The number of units of your product or service you must sell in order to have revenues equal your operating costs for producing that product or service

Identifying other key success factors

Other key success factors besides the breakeven point might include:

- Advantages in sourcing materials. You may have acquired the rights to inexpensive raw materials or discovered a cheaper way of transporting the goods to your facilities. For example, you might have made a deal with the United States Post Office or the local phone company to deliver your message to every household in a certain area.

- Technological innovations in the manufacturing or distribution process. Technological improvements in manufacturing, in transferring information and data, or in organizing distribution systems can lower costs or increase productivity. For example, you may be able to achieve efficient distribution through computerized warehouses communicating with a fleet of delivery trucks.

- **A favorable geographical location.** Depending on the type of business, location can mean success or failure—proximity to customers, competitors, suppliers, or labor supply may be the critical variables. For example, a good location for a food processing plant would be near the growers who raise the crops, and a good location for a computer games arcade might be near a local high school or college.

- **Access to skilled employees or inexpensive labor.** Can you offer recent college graduates internships that would provide the company with inexpensive skilled labor and a pool of experienced employees in the future? Can you provide in-house training to ensure the skilled workforce you need? Can you draw from a large labor pool willing to accept lower wages?

- **An effective pricing strategy.** You may be able to adjust pricing to the needs of individual market segments or match high prices with unique service features. With the technological efficiencies gained in production, you could offer lower prices and still maintain profitable margins.

Remember that your presentation can be simplified and clarified by using detailed flowcharts, process descriptions, and so on, both in the main section and as attachments. Visual aids such as charts, graphs, and tables are useful in presenting complicated information clearly.

Management Summary

E VERY INVESTOR KNOWS that it's the management team, the people, that make a business work. You and your team are the glue that brings the pieces together into a finely formed, dynamic unit. Without the right people, no unique opportunity will move from concept to reality. So, the management summary is an important section of the business plan—one that many of your readers will turn to first.

Describing your team
members' qualifications

The reviewing committee members may already have some acquaintance with you, and, for all types of readers, your résumés will be included in an attachment to the business plan. But here you should answer the more pointed questions those readers—whether they are potential investors, lenders, or internal reviewers—will ask:

- **Where have the team members worked?** What has been their career path, inside the company or beyond? Readers want to know how much experience team members have in the company, in the industry—or related industries—and who their contacts are. Do they have experience that relates directly to this proposed business?

- **What have they accomplished?** What are the team members' achievements? Do they have a record of successfully completing projects? In other words, have they shown that they can take an idea and produce results?

- **What is their reputation in the business community?** Are they known to be idea people who rarely settle down to finish one project before being diverted by another? Do they have a reputation for integrity, living up to their claims? Are they known to be hardworking and dedicated to their work?

- **Are they realistic about the business's chances for success?** Are they capable of recognizing risks and responding to the problems that will inevitably occur? Are their critical assumptions viable? Who on the team will be a visionary? Who will give the word of caution?

- **What knowledge, skills, and special abilities do they bring to the business?** Do members of your management team have a balanced blend of experience, a range of skills, a depth of knowledge? Is the team complete, or does it need to bring in someone else with additional skills or attributes?

- **How committed are they to this venture?** Will they stick with it during the rough times? Have they worked together before on projects? A newly formed collection of people that hasn't been tested as a team is generally considered a riskier proposition than a team that has worked together in the past—a team that has overcome internal conflicts and external problems to attain a defined goal.

- **What are each member's motivations?** What do they hope to achieve? Is each member of the team there by chance or by choice? If they have chosen to be on board, then what benefits do they hope for? If they have been assigned to the team, what motivation do they have to participate and strive for team success?

Introducing the team as a unit

The management summary is your chance to let the reader know how each of the team members will work to form an effective and successful team, which, in turn, will result in a successful and profitable business. Show how this is the right team to manage the risks and to capitalize on the opportunities by:

- **Affirming the team's strengths.** Describe how the skills, knowledge, and experience of the individual team members balance the team as a whole.

- **Acknowledging and addressing the team's perceived weaknesses.** Recognize the management gaps that may exist, such as technical skills or marketing experience. Let the reader know how you plan to deal with these weaknesses or gaps—for example, by training a team member, hiring a new person with the needed skills, or contracting the services of a consulting firm.

- **Expressing the team's management philosophy.** Develop a management philosophy that provides guidelines for each member's behavior and decision-making process. A clear statement of the management philosophy offers an expression of company values and serves as an example of the team's cohesiveness.

Financial
Plan

T HE FINANCIAL PLAN is a critical section of your business plan because it translates all the other parts of the business—the opportunity, the operating plan, the marketing plan, the management team—into anticipated financial results. To prepare this part of your plan, start by thinking about your readers' concerns.

Anticipating readers' concerns

Different readers of your business plan will have different points of view as they approach the financial plan:

- The *investment committee member* reviewing your proposal wants to know whether the venture can achieve the company's hurdle rate (the minimum rate of return expected of all projects).
- The *investor* considering buying into the venture wants to know what kind of return on investment the business will achieve.
- The *lender* deciding whether to approve a loan wants to know about the borrowing capacity of the company, its ability to service debt.
- Perhaps most important, *you* need to know whether your financial objectives will be achieved—whether all your planning and efforts are going to pay off in the end.

This section of your business plan is where you show your readers the current status and future projections of the company's financial performance. The financial picture you paint here represents your best estimate of the risks involved and the return on investment, the tangible evidence of commercial success.

Specifying your business's capital requirements

Whether your project is a business expansion or a new venture, the readers of your business plan will want to know what capital investment is required.

How much money do you need to raise, how much do you expect from them, and how do you intend to use the money?

Tip: Don't plan on overburdening the business with too much debt. Debt can seem attractive—ready cash!—but too much debt can weigh down a company's ability to grow.

For Private Communications Corporation's financial plan, Laszlo opens by stating the capital requirements—how much money they are seeking—and how the money will be used (for system development, marketing expenses, partner acquisition programs, etc.).

Financial Plan

Capital requirements

The Company is presently seeking to raise the sum of Two Hundred and Fifty Thousand Dollars ($250,000). According to current projections, the Company believes that these proceeds, together with Eighty-Four Thousand Dollars ($84,000) the Company has already raised in its initial round of financing, will be sufficient to achieve its business plan. After the first six months of operation, the Company will be able to fund all operation, marketing, and product development costs internally.

The Company intends to use the $334,000 during the first six months of operation, as shown below:

- $45,000 for system development and programming
- $200,000 for marketing expenses
- $89,000 for working capital to fund future product development, promotion, and partner acquisition programs

Summary financial projections

The financial plan portrays a projection of first-year sales of $11.74 million, gross margins over 60 percent, and net margins of approximately 42 percent before tax. The Company expects to be profitable after the first six months of operation and remain profitable from that point on. Other expenses are budgeted as a percentage of revenues according to similar industry ratios. Given these projected numbers, the Company anticipates being profitable and cash flow positive within six months of Product launch. The important results of the financial forecast are summarized below:

	2008	2009	2010	2011	2012
Revenue ($)	11,744,628	33,826,076	39,624,551	43,587,006	47,945,706
Operating profit ($)	4,923,821	14,549,719	16,963,578	18,723,261	20,660,335
Operating margin	42%	43%	43%	43%	43%
Net income ($)	4,922,779	14,547,754	16,963,451	18,723,180	20,660,302
Net margin	42%	43%	43%	43%	43%

Providing financial projections

In this section, you should highlight and explain the importance of the significant figures from the pro forma income statements—revenue, operating profit, operating margin, net income, net margin—over a period of three to five years. State when you expect the company to become profitable.

Tip: Do the number crunching yourself. Even if you are not a numbers person and have expert advice, get in there and do the gritty work of building an income statement and balance sheet.

The pro forma financial statements are projected statements—what you believe will be the future income. They represent your most honest analysis of the financial progress of the business. The income statement, also know as the profit and loss statement, shows the profit margins. The balance sheet provides a picture of the business's assets, equities, and liabilities at a specific point in time.

In addition to the income statement summary, most of your readers will be concerned with the cash flow statement. Including a summary of the flow of cash, showing the times of peak need and peak availability, will demonstrate that your plan has accounted for the variability of cash flows.

Tip: If your new business is a start-up venture, pay especially close attention to cash flow in your financial plan. Although most people think of profits first, cash flow can be more important for a start-up.

Cash flow is often presented on a quarterly or monthly basis.

Articulating your assumptions

State your assumptions about the estimated industry and market growth rates. Then give your assumptions about the internal variables of the business, such as the variable and fixed costs, growth rate of sales, cost of capital, and seasonal cash flow fluctuations.

Your assumptions are the underpinnings of your financial plan. They should be realistic, within the bounds of industry expe-

rience. Include a more detailed set of assumptions as an attachment. Be sure to document your assumptions. Give your sources,
evidence, expert opinions, and your own logic for choosing a certain growth rate or cost for distribution. PCC's assumptions are
show below.

Assumptions

The financial projections are based on current industry estimates of
Internet and proprietary OSP subscribers, primary and secondary
market research data, and estimates of the Product's market penetration and sales growth. More detailed information on the assumptions can be found in the statements prepared for years 2008
through 2012. These statements include projected income statements, balance sheets, and cash flows, as well as a detailed break-
down of assumptions.

Revenues include those resulting from registration of new accounts and sales of additional calling minutes. Cost of goods sold,
while calculated on a per-minute rate, includes all services associated with buying, selling, and billing the customer for long-distance
time, as well as all fees and chargebacks associated with credit card
billing. Marketing and sales expenses include costs associated with
advertising, PR, and promotions, as well as those from revenue sharing with strategic partners. The company will not carry any inven-
tory and will operate with minimal overhead, due to the nature of
the business.

Conducting breakeven analysis for sales

As you saw earlier, the breakeven point is the time when the business is neither losing nor gaining money. This is the pivotal moment when the business begins to be profitable. Will it take six months or two years for the business venture to reach its breakeven? The reader of your business plan will want to know when and at what level of sales the breakeven point will occur.

The breakeven point for sales is calculated as follows:

$$\text{Breakeven} = \frac{\text{Fixed Cost}}{(\text{Sales} - \text{Variable Costs})/\text{Sales}}$$

where fixed costs are those costs that don't change as sales go up or down (for example, rental of facilities), and variable costs vary in proportion to sales (for example, raw materials). This calculation could be included in the attachments to your business plan.

Assessing risk and reward

Risk is the uncertainty of the future. Even with the most careful planning and judicious assumptions, you cannot predict what will happen tomorrow or next month or next year. Planning at all levels—understanding the business environment, developing the operations plan and the marketing plan—is the best way to reduce a venture's exposure to risk, but you can never completely eliminate risk.

There is real risk in any venture—the risk of failure and the possibility of reward. Your readers will want to know your assess-

FIGURE 1

Risk/return graph

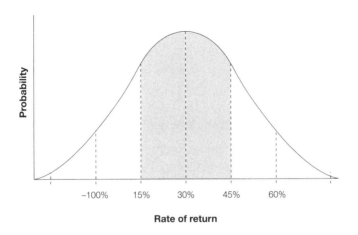

Rate of return

Source: Harvard ManageMentor® on Business Plan Development, adapted with permission.

ment of the level of risk. They want to know how you plan to avoid the risk of failure and how you plan to increase the chances for success. A risk/return graph can quickly show your readers the likelihood of failure, of achieving the predicted levels of return, and the chance of phenomenal success.

The risk/return graph shows investors the probability of possible outcomes. The risk of losing everything is very low, as is the chance of a very high return. The most likely outcome is indicated by the area under the bell curve, ranging from an acceptable (perhaps) return of 15 percent to the most likely return of 30 percent and a possible 45 percent rate of return. Depending on the fundamental riskiness of the venture (drilling for oil is riskier than opening a retail clothes store), the investor will require different rates of return to balance the possibility of loss (an investor investing in oil drilling would expect a high return to compensate for the risk of loss).

Anticipating financial returns

Investors also want to know the expected financial returns—typically either the return on investment (ROI) or the internal rate of return (IRR). For an internal project, the financial return should exceed the company's hurdle rate—the minimum rate of return expected of all projects. For a risky start-up business, investors generally require a higher return to compensate for the higher level of risk of loss.

To calculate the ROI, divide net operating income by total investments. For example:

$$\$45,000 \,/\, \$300,000 = 0.15 \text{ or } 15\% \text{ ROI}$$

The higher the ROI, the more efficient the company is in using its capital to produce a profit.

To calculate an IRR of 50 percent—the return an investor might expect for a risky investment—use the following formula:

$$FV = \text{investment} \times (1 + 0.5)^n$$

where *FV* is future value, *investment* is the dollar amount of the investment, and *n* is the number of years to receive the return.

The complete set of financial information—assumptions, income statements, cash flow statements, balance sheets, statement of sources and uses—should be included in the attachments to your business plan.

Attachments and Milestones

Providing attachments

Attachments come at the end of the business plan and serve a useful purpose of providing additional information for the reader without weighing down the body of the plan. This is the place where you can include the details of the financial plan, the technological specifications of the production plan, and the formal résumés for each member of the management team.

Stipulating milestones

You can also include a milestones plan that lists the major events in the business's development. This serves to give your reader a perspective on the timeline for creating a successful business. To create your milestones plan, apply these strategies:

- Include only major events, not each individual step.

- Choose milestones that can be clearly defined and easily measured—for example, "prototype development," "installation of computer system," "market testing completed," or "first customer sale."

- Use generic dates, such as "month six" or "year one," rather than actual dates.

FIGURE 2

Milestone timeline

- Give yourself room for the unexpected. You never know when a problem will occur that slows you down.

- On the other hand, develop an ambitious schedule that you can meet. This will impress investors and improve your reputation.

Tips and Tools

Tools for
Creating a Business Plan

Pro Forma Financial Package (Introduction)

Contents

Overview

Planning for the future is something managers spend much of their time doing. Marketing plans new products, manufacturing plans material requirements, and finance plans how much money the company needs to operate from day to day. This is where financial forecasting comes in. When a company runs out of money, there is nothing it can do, short of winning the lottery, to sustain itself over the long run. By developing pro forma financial forecasts, managers can estimate their financing requirements and make plans accordingly. Through financial modeling, managers construct "what-if" scenarios by changing model inputs and observing the results, for better or worse. The pro forma model tool helps you build and analyze companies using this approach.

One major use of pro forma forecasting is estimating the future external financing needs of a company. This allows managers to seek out the necessary cash inflows before they impact normal company operations. There are several methods of forecasting financial statements, one of which is the percent-of-sales method. This simple but effective approach involves tying many of the income statement and balance sheet figures to future sales. This system works well because many of the variable costs and most current assets and liabilities vary more-or-less directly with sales. There are exceptions to this rule, but for our purposes (and this model) many of the line items take their cues from the annual growth in sales revenues.

The goal of this tool is to show you an example of a simple pro forma income statement, balance sheet, and cash flow analysis for a business. The results will be simple; for more advanced forecasting, you may need to adopt a more sophisticated financial planning tool. However, this tool will help you develop a solid initial understanding of the economics of a business and forecasting in general.

Before you begin, take a few minutes to look at the various contents of the financial package as a whole. We've provided some sample data to give you a feel for how your results might look when you're done.

Tool Elements

Base Year

This is the starting point for entering data about the company you are analyzing. The model assumes that we are starting a new company; however, the base year can represent the company's first year in existence or the last year of actual data. The rest of the numbers are estimates of the first-year financials.

Assumptions

This page includes an extensive list of assumptions for the model.

Income Statement - Balance Sheet - Cash Flow

These are the primary output reports of our base year and assumption inputs.

Income Statement Chart - Balance Sheet Chart
Cash Flow Chart - Cumulative Free Cash Flow Chart

These charts reflect the output on each of the associated reports.

Pro Forma Financial Package (Base Year)

Enter data in thousands of dollars

Base Year	2007

Income Statement

Revenue	2,000
Annual Revenue Growth Rate	20%
Total Cost of Goods Sold	900
Gross Margin	1,100
Sales Expenses	300
Marketing Expenses	100
General and Admin. Expenses	100
Other Expenses 1	0
Other Expenses 2	0
Other Expenses 3	0
Other Expenses 4	0
Total Operating Expenses	500
Depreciation Assumption	5 Year—Straight Line
Depreciation Expense	200
Operating Profit	400
Other Income (Expense)	0
Interest Income	3
Interest Expense	16
Pre-Tax Income	387
Income Tax Rate	20%
Income Tax	77
Net Income	310
Preferred Dividends	0
Common Dividends	0

Balance Sheet

As of	12/31/07
Assets	
Operating Cash	50
Marketable Securities	60
Accounts Receivable	80
Inventory	40
Other Current Assets	100
Total Current Assets	330
Gross Plant & Equipment	1,000
Accumulated Depreciation	100
Net Plant & Equipment	900
Other Long-Term Assets	100
Total Long-Term Assets	1,000
Total Assets	1,330
Liabilities	
Accounts Payable	50
Short-Term Debt	80
Current Maturities	15
Taxes Payable	5
Other Current Liabilities	40
Total Current Liabilities	190
Long-Term Debt	120
Term of Long-Term Debt	8 Years
Other Long-Term Liabilities	65
Total Long-Term Liabilities	185
Preferred Stock	0
Common Surplus	455
Retained Earnings	0
Shareholders Equity	455
Total Liabilities and Shareholders' Equity	830

Cash Flow Analysis

Capital Expenditures	500
Interest Income Rate	5%
Interest Expense Rate (Short-Term)	8%
Interest Expense Rate (Long-Term)	7%

Pro Forma Financial Package (Assumptions)

	Base Year	Year 1	Year 2	Year 3	Year 4	Year 5
	2007	2008	2009	2010	2011	2012
Annual Revenue Growth Rate		20.0%	20.0%	20.0%	20.0%	20.0%
Revenue	2,000	2,400	2,880	3,456	4,147	4,977
Cost of Goods Sold as a % of Revenue	45.0%	45.0%	45.0%	45.0%	45.0%	45.0%
Sales Expenses	15.0%	15.0%	15.0%	15.0%	15.0%	15.0%
Marketing Expenses	5.0%	5.0%	5.0%	5.0%	5.0%	5.0%
General and Admin. Expenses	5.0%	5.0%	5.0%	5.0%	5.0%	5.0%
Other Expenses 1	0.0%	0.0%	0.0%	0.0%	0.0%	0.0%
Other Expenses 2	0.0%	0.0%	0.0%	0.0%	0.0%	0.0%
Other Expenses 3	0.0%	0.0%	0.0%	0.0%	0.0%	0.0%
Other Expenses 4	0.0%	0.0%	0.0%	0.0%	0.0%	0.0%
Other Income (Expense) as a % of Revenue	0.0%	0.0%	0.0%	0.0%	0.0%	0.0%
Interest Income Rate	5.0%	5.0%	5.0%	5.0%	5.0%	5.0%
Interest Expense Rate (Short-Term)	8.0%	8.0%	8.0%	8.0%	8.0%	8.0%
Interest Expense Rate (Long-Term)	7.0%	7.0%	7.0%	7.0%	7.0%	7.0%
Income Tax Rate	20.0%	20.0%	20.0%	20.0%	20.0%	20.0%
Preferred Dividend Rate	0.0%	0.0%	0.0%	0.0%	0.0%	0.0%
Common Dividend Payout Ratio	0.0%	0.0%	0.0%	0.0%	0.0%	0.0%
Operating Cash as a % of Revenue	2.5%	2.5%	2.5%	2.5%	2.5%	2.5%
Accounts Receivable as a % of Revenue	4.0%	4.0%	4.0%	4.0%	4.0%	4.0%
Days Receivable	15	15	15	15	15	15
Inventory as a % of Cost of Goods Sold	4.4%	4.4%	4.4%	4.4%	4.4%	4.4%
Inventory Days	16	16	16	16	16	16
Other Current Assets as a % of Revenue	5.0%	5.0%	5.0%	5.0%	5.0%	5.0%
Capital Expenditures	500	380	452	546	667	822
Other Long-Term Assets as a % of Revenue	5.0%	5.0%	5.0%	5.0%	5.0%	5.0%

	Base Year	Year 1	Year 2	Year 3	Year 4	Year 5
	2007	2008	2009	2010	2011	2012
Accounts Payable as a % of COGS	5.6%	5.6%	5.6%	5.6%	5.6%	5.6%
Days Payable	20	20	20	20	20	20
Short-Term Debt	80	80	80	80	80	80
Current Maturities of Long-Term Debt	15	15	15	15	15	15
Long-Term Debt	120	105	90	75	60	45
Taxes Payable as a % of Taxes	6.5%	6.5%	6.5%	6.5%	6.5%	6.5%
Other Current Liabilities as a % of Revenue	2.0%	2.0%	2.0%	2.0%	2.0%	2.0%
Other Long-Term Liabilities as a % of Revenue	3.3%	3.3%	3.3%	3.3%	3.3%	3.3%
Preferred Stock	0	0	0	0	0	0
Common Surplus	455	455	455	455	455	455

Depreciation Tables: Assumes: 5 Year—Straight Line

Year	Capital Expenditures	Base Year	1	2	3	4	5	6
1	380			76	76	76	76	76
2	452				90	90	90	90
3	546					109	109	109
4	667						133	133
5	822							164
Depreciation for the Year			200	236	286	356	449	573
Net Plant & Equipment	900	1,080	1,296	1,555	1,866	2,239	0	

Pro Forma Financial Package (Income Statement)

Data shown in thousands of dollars

	Base Year	Year 1	Year 2	Year 3	Year 4	Year 5
	2007	2008	2009	2010	2011	2012
Revenue	2,000	2,400	2,880	3,456	4,147	4,977
Cost of Goods Sold	900	1,080	1,296	1,555	1,866	2,239
Gross Margin	1,100	1,320	1,584	1,901	2,281	2,737
Sales Expenses	300	360	432	518	622	746
Marketing Expenses	100	120	144	173	207	249
General and Admin. Expenses	100	120	144	173	207	249
Other Expenses 1	0	0	0	0	0	0
Other Expenses 2	0	0	0	0	0	0
Other Expenses 3	0	0	0	0	0	0
Other Expenses 4	0	0	0	0	0	0
Total Operating Expenses	500	600	720	864	1,037	1,244
Depreciation Expense	200	236	286	356	449	573
Operating Profit	400	484	578	681	795	920
Other Income (Expense)	0	0	0	0	0	0
Interest Income	3	2	0	1	8	20
Interest Expense	16	28	33	19	12	11
Pre-Tax Income	387	458	545	663	791	929
Income Tax	77	92	109	133	158	186
Net Income	310	366	436	530	633	743
Preferred Dividends	0	0	0	0	0	0
Common Dividends	0	0	0	0	0	0

Pro Forma Financial Package (Balance Sheet)

Data shown in thousands of dollars

	Base Year	Year 1	Year 2	Year 3	Year 4	Year 5
	2007	2008	2009	2010	2011	2012
Assets						
Operating Cash	50	60	72	86	104	124
Marketable Securities	60	0	0	39	273	541
Accounts Receivable	80	96	115	138	166	199
Inventory	40	48	58	69	83	100
Other Current Assets	100	120	144	173	207	249
Total Current Assets	330	324	389	505	833	1,212
Net Plant & Equipment	900	1,080	1,296	1,555	1,866	2,239
Other Long-Term Assets	100	120	144	173	207	249
Total Long-Term Assets	1,000	1,200	1,440	1,728	2,074	2,488
Total Assets	1,330	1,524	1,829	2,233	2,906	3,701
Liabilities						
Accounts Payable	50	60	72	86	104	124
Short-Term Debt	80	80	80	80	80	80
Current Maturities	15	15	15	15	15	15
Taxes Payable	5	6	7	9	10	12
Other Current Liabilities	40	48	58	69	83	100
Total Current Liabilities	190	209	232	259	292	331
Long-Term Debt	120	105	90	75	60	45
Other Long-Term Liabilities	65	78	94	112	135	162
Total Long-Term Liabilities	185	183	184	187	195	207
Surplus Liabilities	0	311	157	0	0	0
Preferred Stock	0	0	0	0	0	0
Common Surplus	455	455	455	455	455	455
Retained Earnings	0	366	802	1,332	1,965	2,708
Shareholders' Equity	455	821	1,257	1,787	2,420	3,163
Total Liabilities & Shareholders' Equity	830	1,524	1,829	2,233	2,906	3,701
In-Balance Test	500	0	0	0	0	0

Pro Forma Financial Package (Cash Flow)

Data shown in thousands of dollars

	Base Year	Year 1	Year 2	Year 3	Year 4	Year 5
	2007	2008	2009	2010	2011	2012
Revenues	2,000	2,400	2,880	3,456	4,147	4,977
Earnings Before Interest & Taxes	400	484	578	681	795	920
Less Tax Exposure	80	97	116	136	159	184
Earnings Before Interest & After Taxes	320	387	462	545	636	736
Plus Depreciation	200	236	286	356	449	573
Operating Cash Flow	520	623	748	901	1,085	1,309
Operating Working Capital	175	210	252	302	363	436
Less Increase (Decrease) in Operating Working Capital	0	35	42	50	61	73
Plus Increase (Decrease) in Other Long-Term Liabilities	0	13	16	19	22	27
Less Increase (Decrease) in Other Long-Term Assets	0	20	24	29	35	41
Less Capital Expenditures	500	380	452	546	667	822
Free Cash Flow	20	201	246	295	346	400
Less After-Tax Interest Expense (Income)	10	21	26	15	4	(7)
Less Amortization of Debt	15	15	15	15	15	15
Less Total Dividends	0	0	0	0	0	0
External Financing Surplus (Deficit)		165	205	265	327	392

Pro Forma Financial Package (Income Statement Chart)

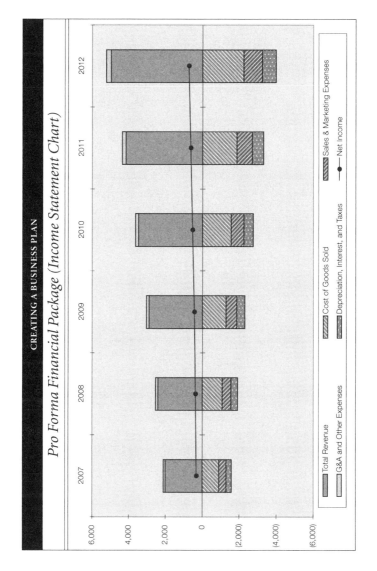

Pro Forma Financial Package (Balance Sheet Chart)

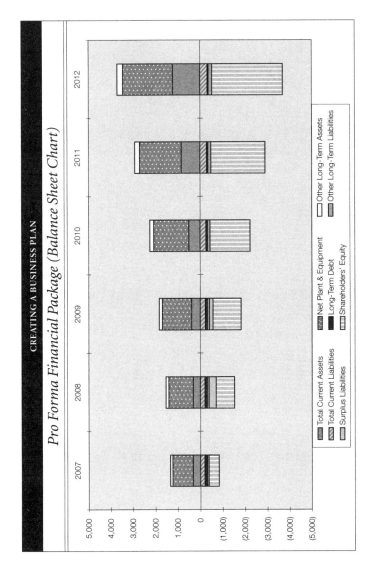

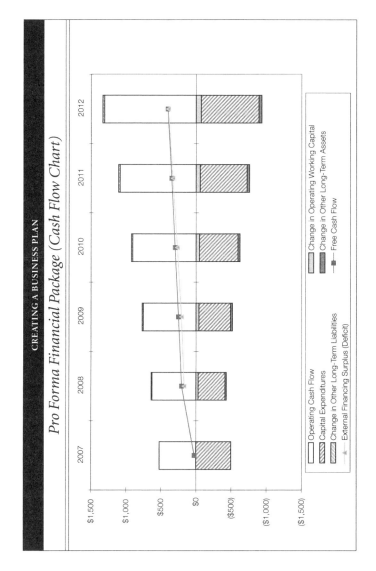

Pro Forma Financial Package (Cash Flow Chart)

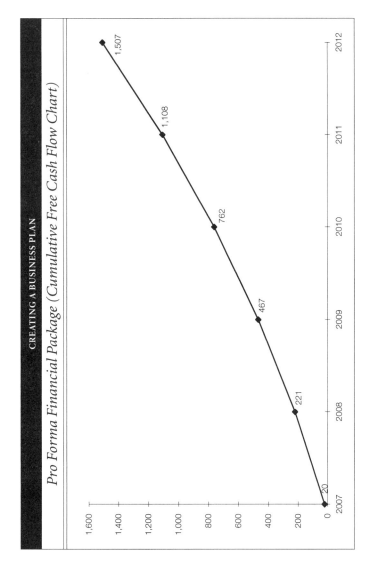

Pro Forma Financial Package (Cumulative Free Cash Flow Chart)

Test Yourself

This section offers ten multiple-choice questions to help you identify your baseline knowledge of business plan essentials. Answers to the questions are given at the end of the test.

1. The executive summary portion of your business plan is best written after you draft the rest of the plan. True or false?

　a. True.

　b. False.

2. You're drafting a business plan and have defined who your colleagues and competitors will be. You're providing information on which of the following?

　a. The market.

　b. The marketing mix.

　c. The industry.

3. The area of overlap between analysis of the industry and the market is called:

　a. Business opportunity.

　b. Distribution channel.

　c. Promotion strategy.

4. The part of the business plan that details the daily flow of activities and work of the business, such as how raw materials will be turned into finished goods to be sold, is called the:

   a. Management summary.

   b. Marketing plan.

   c. Business description.

   d. Operations plan.

5. _____ is the minimum rate of return that is expected of all projects in a company.

   a. Hurdle rate.

   b. Gross margin.

   c. Return on investment.

6. A financial tool that could help you show the point at which your business or venture is expected to neither be losing money nor making money is a:

   a. Balance sheet.

   b. Breakeven analysis.

   c. Cash flow analysis.

7. The parts of the financial plan that show the profit margins you expect your business to achieve are the:

   a. Pro forma income statements.

   b. Balance sheets.

8. When you are developing the milestones portion of your business plan, it is generally advisable to do all of the following *except*:

   a. Include only major events, not every individual step.

   b. Use actual dates.

   c. Leave time in the schedule for the unexpected.

   d. Develop an ambitious schedule you can meet.

9. When you are writing the business description part of your business plan, it is advisable to maintain a businesslike tone and to avoid infusing the summary with your own enthusiasm. True or false?

   a. True.

   b. False.

10. A business plan is typically written once to secure funding and is not the type of plan to be monitored or updated, since it cannot help direct operations. True or false?

   a. True.

   b. False.

Answers to test questions

1, a. Since the executive summary should be a concise presentation of the major points in your business plan, it is best written last. If you were to write it at the beginning, you probably would end up making significant revisions later.

2, c. The industry is the group of companies that produces and sells products or services to the market, so it determines who your colleagues and competitors will be.

3, a. The terms *industry* and *market* describe parts of the total business environment. The area of intersection between industry and market represents your business opportunity—that space in which the customer need and the product or service meet.

4, d. The operations plan should show how work would be accomplished, with a focus on the critical operating factors that will make your proposed business a success.

5, a. If a project or venture doesn't pass the company's hurdle rate, it may not get approved or funded.

6, b. The breakeven point is the pivotal time when a business can begin to earn a profit. Readers of business plans want to know when and at what level of sales the breakeven point will occur. Breakeven analysis enables you to provide that information.

7, a. Pro forma income statements represent your most honest analysis of the financial progress of the business. Income statements, also known as profit and loss statements, show expected profit margins as well as revenue, operating margin, and net income.

8, b. It is generally not advisable to use actual dates in the milestone portion of your business plan. Instead, you should use generic dates, such as six months or one year, rather than actual dates. Specific dates are not always needed, and they leave you less room for maneuvering than generic dates.

9, b.   While you want to use a professional, businesslike tone in the business description part of your business plan, this part also provides you with an opportunity to incorporate some of your enthusiasm and conviction that this business concept will be a successful venture. It's a chance for you present the value of your concept—why you believe the business will be a success.

10, b.   While some people may perceive the business plan as a static document that is written once and then put on the shelf, it is very appropriate to routinely monitor it and update it to help track the progress of your business.

To Learn More

Notes and Articles

Harvard Business School Publishing. "Starting New Businesses—Inside the Organization." *Harvard Management Update* (December 1999).

> Intrapreneurship isn't exactly new—the concept of creating new businesses within large companies was briefly popular in the 1980s, but most companies soon became too concerned with reengineering and downsizing to look for new business opportunities. These days, however, intrapreneurship is back. Companies are leaner and are looking for ways to grow and to survive in an increasingly competitive marketplace. Intrapreneurship goes beyond the production of ideas to actually foster new ventures—it requires training and coaching, incentives, and buy-in from senior levels to ensure that new businesses can really emerge.

Sahlman, William A. "How to Write a Great Business Plan." *Harvard Business Review* (July–August 1997).

> Most business plans pour far too much ink on the numbers—and far too little on the information that *really* matters: the

people, the opportunity, the context, and the possibilities for both risk and reward. This article builds on Sahlman's "Some Thoughts on Business Plans," showing managers how to pose—and answer—the right questions in preparing their business plans.

Books

Bangs, David H. *The Business Planning Guide: Creating a Plan for Success in Your Own Business.* 8th ed. Chicago: Upstart Publishing Company, 1998.

Forbes magazine named this book as its favorite, most useful small-business resource. This new edition includes information on using the Internet as a business-planning tool.

Covello, Joseph, and Brian Hazelgren. *Your First Business Plan.* 3rd ed. Naperville, IL: Sourcebooks, 1998.

This guide to writing a business plan includes an interactive, step-by-step process that focuses on the USA (Unique Selling Advantage). It includes a model of a complete business plan and a glossary of terms.

Pinson, Linda, and Jerry Jinnett. *Anatomy of a Business Plan: A Step-by-Step Guide to Starting Smart, Building the Business, and Securing Your Company's Future.* 4th ed. Chicago: Dearborn Financial Publishing, 1999.

This award-winning best seller has helped more than five hundred thousand people write business plans that work. Provides step-by-step instructions for creating a polished, professional, and results-oriented plan, as well as plenty of sample forms, worksheets, examples, and two complete plans to use as models. Includes the latest Web-marketing strategies and other recent resources available to entrepreneurs.

eLearning Products

Harvard Business School Publishing. *Case in Point*. Boston: Harvard Business School Publishing, 2004.

Case in Point is a flexible set of online cases, designed to help prepare middle- and senior-level managers for a variety of leadership challenges. These short, reality-based scenarios provide sophisticated content to create a focused view into the realities of the life of a leader. Your managers will experience aligning strategy, removing implementation barriers, overseeing change, anticipating risk, ethical decisions, building a business case, cultivating customer loyalty, emotional intelligence, developing a global perspective, fostering innovation, defining problems, selecting solutions, managing difficult interactions, fulfilling the coach's role, delegating for growth, managing creativity, influencing others, managing performance, providing feedback, and retaining talent.

Sources for Creating a Business Plan

We would like to acknowledge the sources who aided in developing this topic.

Covello, Joseph, and Brian Hazelgren. *Your First Business Plan.* 3rd ed. Naperville, IL: Sourcebooks, 1998.

DeThomas, Arthur R., PhD, and William B. Fredenberger, PhD. *Writing a Convincing Business Plan.* Hauppauge, NY: Barron's, 1995.

Gumpert, David E. *How to Really Create a Successful Business Plan: Step-by-Step Guide.* Boston: Inc. Publishing, 1996.

HBS Toolkit. Boston: Harvard Business School, 1999.

Sahlman, William A. "How to Write a Great Business Plan." *Harvard Business Review* (July–August 1997).

Sahlman, William A. "Some Thoughts on Business Plans." Case Note 9-897-101. Boston: Harvard Business School, November 1996.

Siegel, Eric S., Brian R. Ford, and Jay M. Bornstein. *The Ernst & Young Business Plan Guide.* New York: Wiley, 1993.